The Beauty Within the Vessel: Poetry from a troubled youth

Copyright © 2016 by Matthew Williams

All rights reserved. No part of this publication may be reproduced, distributed, or transmitted in any form or by any means without the prior written permission of the author. For permission requests, questions or concerns, call the publisher "Poetae Publishing".

Poetae Publishing

Philadelphia, Pa 19139

Contact:

http://www.poetaepublishing.com/

Thanks and Dedication

I would like to thank everybody who was with me through this long journey. My countless number of friends who have read every single poem I have ever written, both good and bad. I would like to thank my family for their love and support, especially when times got rough. I would like to also thank the people who really motivated me to get my book published, my mother and sister, the Dennis family, Jazmine Renee who wrote an incredible foreword for me, Travis Smith, Susan Delp, countless teachers, family, friends and everybody in-between.

I like to give thanks and praise to God, without whom this book would not be possible.

This book is dedicated:

~ to all of the dreamers in this world. Don't ever let anybody try to silence your dreams. Dream loud, and make the world listen.

~and to the generation coming after me, Cianni, Enya, Kaylin, Myleena , Kiera, Brandon, Bryce, Christian, Amir,

Quadir, Jonathan and many many others. The future is yours for the taking.

Foreword

Words.

This book will begin much like other books out there. With words. But if you allow me, I'll use those words to make meanings and feelings flutter off of the page and into you heart, mind and soul.

Poetry is never a meaningless entity. It is much like the modern working woman who walks with purpose and holds her head high. Poetry is the order that brings chaos to rest in its noisy, messy tracks. She brings to the table the calm of meditation, the blunt attitude of a battered soul and everything in between. Through a poem, one can glimpse into the soul of another and entwine themselves in the thoughts, feelings, and emotions as a child would under a blanket on a cold night. Poetry's purpose seeks to acknowledge the injustices of the world, both small and large, while delivering them in beautiful gift wrapping.

This book is the gift wrapping that will deliver the ordered chaos that is the mind of the author.

To have spent several years as a close friend of Matthew is a once in a lifetime experience. I have been given the chance to experience laughter, tears, joy, and happiness with an artist that paints the world beautifully with words. We have leaned on each other through it all and the most important thing that this book will do is provide a chance for you to connect with the bright light that has already touched many lives, including my own.

The most distinguishable trait about Matthew is his selflessness. To give and give in this world can be discouraging and difficult, especially for an artist. However, that has not stopped him from sharing his work with those of us who struggle to find that selflessness and talent within ourselves.

As an artist, it is fleeting to tackle your art and produce excellence. Though we may face difficulties along the way, it is an accomplishment that inspires those around us.

"Jazzy, I'm going to take a break from poetry for a while"

This is a conversation I will always remember. To see an artist feel the frustration of his art so much so that it must take a back seat is painful. As a friend, it is similar to a falling dream that one cannot escape. How can I pull you away from the darkness without losing both of us? Though the darkness may fight the good fight frequently in our lives, this day helped me make an important promise to myself and my best friend. Always believe in something no matter where life takes you. I will always believe in Matthew, and I have promised myself to never let him give up and to inspire Matthew the way he inspires me every day.

> "If I read a book and it makes my whole body so cold no fire could ever warm me, I know *that* is poetry."
>
> -Emily Dickinson

~Written by Jazmine Renee. ~

Introduction

"Faber est quisque fortunae suae". In English, this translates into every man is the architect of his own future. This was the motto of my high school. This motto has fueled my passions for education, especially for writing, consistently throughout my college experience. Being the architect of my own future meant shaping my own path, understanding that the outcome of my life is not predetermined, that my future is constantly changing, thinking on my feet, and welcoming adversity with open arms. Two years ago, the notion of me writing a book was one that would cause me to laugh hysterically. It was not something I thought was achievable. Yet, here I am, two books in hand and the future before me, anxiously anticipating what I will do next. After my first publication I was told by a friend that poetry was dead or, at best, on a respirator clinging onto dear life. If that is the truth, then this book will be the defibrillator, poetry the patient and I the doctor. The *Beauty within the Vessel: Poetry from a Troubled Youth* is a book of poetry written as I navigated my senior year through college. With every poem I write, I hope to bring a unique voice and style to the genre of poetry, one that focuses on trying to make poetry engaging and modern, while trying to hold on to the classic techniques of form and style. As you take this journey into my world, you will read poems about my experiences trying to find purpose in life: negotiating relationships, transitions, loss, faith and the ultimate struggle of becoming an "adult."

Table of Contents

A City from tears: pg1

Memories of the city of tears: pg3

Wonderland: pg6

Songs of time: pg9

Single black mother: pg12

Until soon: pg16

Goodbye old friend: pg18

A letter to my eight year old self: pg20

Baby boy: pg24

Dreamer: pg29

Foil: pg33

Love Lost: pg35

The death of the mask: pg37

Warrior Nation: pg40

The seed: pg42

Unnamed: pg43

A prayer for the weary: pg46

Thoughts: pg47

Imagine: pg49

Curse me: pg52

I am the poem: pg45

The Genie's lamp: pg56

Butterfly: pg58

The Fallen Star: 61

Be my siren!: 62

Angel at midnight: 64

The ugly duckling: 69

The caged bird: 72

The mocking bird: 76

The girl no one knows: 80

Outrunning time: 81

Perception: 87

Lullaby: 89

Punch like a man: 91

Colored free: 93

The tears that nurture: 94

Formless: 96

My Secret: 99

A prayer for the Phoenix: 104

A city from tears
(From *The Poet's Song: Poetry from a troubled Youth*)

My city was born,
from the tears of the young.
Slow.
Steady.
Loud.
Impatient.
Filled with hopes that will always fly,
and dreams that will never leave the ground.
Beat boxes,
jump ropes,
men searching through trash cans
to quench their thirst.
That's my city.
A city where art is displayed on sidewalks
not in museums.
Where music pulses through the veins of the living,
and jump starts the bodies of the victims of no rhythm.
My city is filled with break dancers,
filthy streets,
gardens of teddy bears,
and chalk outlines struck frozen
next to pictures of casualties of an endless war.
I live where children are armed right out of the womb,
where the elderly wear glasses
to see the shadows of their past,
and the sun never sets.
I come from a place of immortality,

of kings and queens shrouded in darkness.
A place where time is just another body in the street,
and death walks hand and hand with life.
My city is plastered with smiles,
and it rains stars every night.
Where love is everywhere, but impossible to see,
and my city is growing.
It thrives off of the souls of the ambitious,
it thrives from the imagination of every age,
there are no limits my city can't break,
and no worlds it can't explore,
for my city was born
from the tears of a child.

Memories of the city born from tears

She asked me if I had forgotten her,
the touch of her kiss as I hopped along the streets
to miss Mary Mack,
the jingle of running through the concrete jungle,
jumping over ropes like Jack did candle sticks,
the quenching taste of a hug,
block parties busting at the seams of every corner,
line dancing with ancestors once forgotten,
climbing the bars of my childhood fears,
being thrown into an unexpected world
of curiosity and wonder
as my front wheels kept spinning
but the back ones lost with the bodies piling up
waiting for time to come along
and add them to her collection.
She smiled,
reflecting the memories that faintly linger in my own smile
of the taste of a cheesesteak with extra fried onions,

sweet wooder ice,

apple butter,

freshly planted rose bushes,

broken words created to fix broken people,

catholic schools shrouded in Baptist beliefs,

and homemade deep fried chicken.

I once told her that she was born,

Slow.

Steady.

Loud.

Impatient.

Filled with hopes that will always fly,

and dreams that will never leave the ground.

Beat boxes,

jump ropes,

men searching through trash cans

to quench their thirst.

filthy streets,

gardens of teddy bears,

and chalk outlines struck frozen

next to pictures of casualties of an endless war.

I live where children are armed right out of the womb,

where the elderly wear glasses

to see the shadows of their past,

and the sun never sets.

I come from a place of immortality,

of kings and queens shrouded in darkness.

A place where time is just another body in the street,

and death walks hand and hand with life.

I once said she was born

from the tears of a child,

but children must grow up.

She asked if I will miss her,

If I'll ever call her on the phone

and say I love you.

I laugh,

take her by the hand

and let her see my tears,

for I will always be her child.

Wonderland

He kisses you,
ya'll hands entangled,
African beauty,
royalty.
He pulls you near,
and all I can do is stare.
I thought if I explored your world,
played in the pools of your imagination
you would notice me
not flee…
See,
I was late,
so very late
to this race to your heart,
for he had a head start,
but I had a rabbits foot
and the tick tocking of time in my hand,
reminding me that I was late,
but could I still make you see what you meant to me?
So I ran,
jumping into the hole in your heart
expecting to fit in perfectly, like a key
turn me
and Ill unlock your heart,
as easy as eat me
drink me,
but it was an impossible dream
and breakfast had already past,

and you've reached your limit of impossible things.
But I wanted you,
so I went deeper and deeper,
not seeing the traps you've set,
the games you wanted me to play,
checkmate!
You thought you've won,
another poor soul wanting to know you,
to love you,
but too afraid to fight for you,
except,
I was willing to get lost for you,
cry for you,
loose my reflection in the mirror,
my identity,
who am I?
who are you?
All if it meant loving you, painting the world red for you,
the color of strength,
love,
my heart, my queen,
please take my heart,
hold it and know
that I never want to go,
to grow apart,
to sway,
but rather I wish to stay
forever in your dreams,
your fantasy,
your world,
but the ticking of this clock
keeps reminding me I am late.

I am late.
I will never be your date,
only a shadow,
smiling,
wishing I had known you sooner,
that your fantasy was my reality,
but it can never be.
So I watch,
tip my hat,
my disguise,
disappear,
and stare
as he pulls you near.
Royalty.
African beauty.
Ya'll hands entangled.
He kisses you,
and I cry,
knowing you will be happy.

~Inspired by Lewis Carroll's *Alice in Wonderland*, 1865

Songs of time

You told me to be honest

To be willing to give this a try

Us a try

For someday I might call you from my heart

But I'll be one second too late

Left to talk to the moon

Constantly trying to get to you

Hoping that you're talking to the moon too

Or perhaps I could just find you in my dreams

The place I would have to go to see your beautiful face

again

Cause I realize I'm not over you

Missing you

You're the best thing I never knew I needed

And finally I'm forced to face the truth

That I may have called you one second too late

Cause I can count on you like 4,3,2 you'll be there

My friend

And I want you to count on me like 1,2,3

To be that something again

But I'm scared to say it aloud

Worried that my time has passed

That my moon has set

My table will always be set for 2 even if it's just me

No more 1,2,3

Just one

So I'll wait

And wonder

Pounder

Pray

Stay

Hope my love will never fade away

But for you kid I will stay

Because having you in my life

Even as a friend

Is better than all the riches in the end

~Inspired by:

Ne-Yo "Never knew I needed"

James Morrison "You give me something"

Bruno Mars "Talking to the moon"

Gavin DeGraw "Not over you"

~I do not own any of these songs, but rather used these songs to construct a poem for someone who will always be important and special in my life.

Single black mother

Single black mother
I hear your cry
I hear your prayers
When you've asked why?
Single black mother
I call my own
I have seen you struggle
As I have grown

I remember you rocking me in your arms, holding me tight, as you wiped the tears from my eyes. It was the day I realized I didn't have a father. The day you told me that I didn't need one. You said, hush little baby don't say a word, mommas gona buy you a mocking bird. And if that mocking bird don't sing….Well, then I will do it. You must trust in me, as I put my trust in God for the both of us until you can trust in him on your own. Your words fell upon death ears. Too young to understand the promise you have made, but wise enough to know I could trust you. And I did.

Single black mother
Where is your smile?
Show me your compassion
Let your love stay a while
Single black mother
Hear me when I say
That your struggle is almost over
That soon you can rejoice in a new day

One foot in front of the other, you walked. Pain surging up your back, slowly creeping through your spine, trying to break every bone in your body. Yet, you still smile. When they told you you would be on disability for the rest of your life, you cried. Crying out to God. I have seen the tears when you're in pain. And have heard you sing over and over again, lean on me son when you are not strong, I will be your friend, and I will help you carry on. And you did.

Single black mother
Where is the mask that grins and lies
It doesn't hide your cheeks or shades your eyes
Single black mother
Dunbar got it wrong
Just because you are in pain
Don't mean you are not strong

They've talked about you. Lied on you. Said you would never amount to anything. You would never be anything. Single black teenager mother. Cursed at your name. Cursed at mine. You whispered in my ear, telling me I could do whatever I wanted to do, be whatever I wanted to be because you believed in me. That your success would come in giving me everything you never had. Everything you ever wanted. Everything you ever needed. And it did.

Single black mother
Wipe your eyes
For you are beautiful
And o so wise
Single black mother the top is near
Hang on a little while longer

You'll soon have nothing to fear

When I told you I was leaving you cried. I could hear the pain in your voice, though I could feel the love in your arms. Hug me. Hold me. When I got my college acceptance letter you was terrified. Here, your son was leaving. And yet, you smiled. Knowing, praying, wishing, hoping, nothing but the best for me. Your faith, your promise, your struggle was giving me everything you never had, everything you ever wanted. Everything you ever needed. I was afraid to leave you. To leave my family. But you said you was proud of me. That God would protect me. That my faith must be like a mustard seed. That my faith must be so strong that when I prayed on pebbles mountains would move. You sung loudly, that I could not give up now. That you have come too far from where you started from. That nobody told us the road would be easy, but that we come this far by faith and that you would always be there for me. And you were.

> Single black mother
> Rest easy and relax
> For all you've ever wanted
> Is coming back
> Single black mother
> Your job may never be done
> But you're not alone
> This I promise you as your son

Though the future is a mystery, and the past our history, this present were living in is a gift, one I'll never take it for granted. Take you for granted. I pray every day that your love will never go away. That I can repay in any and every way, every day, all that you have given away to help me grow. See me go. And hopeful one day I'll show you, be a blessing for you, to put on display the fruits of your labor. Thank you, single black mother, thank you.

>   Single black mother
>   I love you this I say
>   With all of my heart
>   And soul everyday
>   Single black mother
>   A gift from above
>   Thank you for loving me
>   For it is you, truly, who I love

Until soon

I never thought I would miss a storm,

The roar of thunder rolling across the sky.

Boom! Boom! Boom! Boom!

Calling for my attention….

The streaks of lightning,

Dancing across the earth with each,

Strike! Strike! Flash! Strike!

Hoping to illuminate my paths,

Trying to show me the wrath of my future,

Unless I instilled hope in the present…

The cascading blessings waiting to flood the earth,

But were buried deep within my soul,

Too afraid to let them be free,

Too afraid of success…

The storm,

Boom, Boom, Boom, Boom, strike, strike, flash, strike….

But now the storm has stopped

And I wonder why I took you for granted,

But hear my screams, yells, cheers,

Rolling off my tongue

Like thunder booming from my soul.

The tears cascading down my face like a flood,

As my hands rip through the air,

Back and forth

Back and forth

Like lightning dancing across the sky,

As the words silently creep from parted lips,

Until we meet again old friend…

Until soon!

Goodbye old friend

I knew I never loved you,
but I hoped that my lustful desire
would hopefully lead me to
a higher level of lust,
so I kissed you gently hoping to gain your trust,
out of fear that if I let you go
I would never find such lust again,
a man made fragile passion.
But I should have let you go.
I sold myself short, never to know,
my true worth,
but now it's too late for goodbye.
The love I wanted has gone away to die,
and I,
I sit
trapped in this lustful pit
of lies and tears,
and all out of fear,

out of lust,

a lustful desire I would hope lead me to you,

the one I knew I never loved.

A letter to my eight year old self

Hush little baby don't say a word
Not one word
Just hush
He said
Yanking my pants from my waist
Shhhhhh
It will only take one second
One second
One second
One second
Stuck on repeat
Replay
Over and over engraved in my 8 year old mind
Mind
I minded
Did I mind?
He told me I didn't
That this was what I wanted
That it was okay
To just hush
Hush and remain silent
Silenced
Struck scared
To silent to say anything
Hoping that my silence was loud enough
A scream echoing in a dark and empty room
echoing
Help me
Help me

Help me
Me
Just eight
What did I do to deserve this
Seven years later I tried to forgive you
But I could never
Can never
Forget
For six months I lied
Hoping
Praying it was a dream
Hoping that one of the Five different counselors
Would have a cure
But there was none
No magic bullet to put me out of my misery
Four, for I was getting tired
Exhausted
Praying to
Three
Father
Son
And spirit
Begging to know why this happened
Two, to me
Why me
Why
Why
No one was there to save me
Just me
one
Alone
It was silent

I was silent
Hushing my sobs

Baby boy
I wish I could take away the pain
The memories
To tell you the road ahead was easy
Worth it
But it's hard
It hurts
But keep your faith
For one day it will be your greatest tool
Even if
Two, today it don't seem like it because
There is power in God's name
Three
Father son and spirit
his spirit
Is deep within you
Four, forever and ever
He has seen the tears you've cried
And he will be there to comfort you
Through those
Five counselors and
And Six months you've lied
he was by your side
Seven days a week
He watched over you
Kept you safe and he was never late
So let your clock strike eight
Because your blessings will come full circle my child
I know

I believe it
I've seen it
I've lived it
I am you
I have survived
We have survived
And trust me
We will thrive

Baby boy

I am sorry. I am sorry that everybody is trying to tell you what boys are. Who boys are.

Boys are loud

Boys are stupid

Boys are proud

Boys are rough

Boys are immature

Boys are tough

Boys lie

Boys cheat

Boys never cry

Just be a man. Tighten up. Grow up. Grow up to be everything but who you want to be, who you are. Be the man we define, and perhaps you will go far. But what if? What if they saw you for who you are, and most importantly, who you could be? What if, baby boy, they let the world be your canvass, your dreams be your paintbrushes, and your imagination be your paint. Are they afraid of what you would create? Instead, they hand you the blueprints to your life, already colored in with monochromatic shades of black and white, because boys shouldn't dream in color.

They will raise you like cattle, the most valuable stock, praying you will become the best fit. The one who will provide the most meat. Money. Power. Substance. They will measure your masculinity in how threating you can be. They will measure your masculinity in how much you can contribute to their own lives because that is what you have been breed for.

You have been breed to be loud, which makes you intimidating and threatening. Remember people always listen to the loudest voice, until they find a way to drown you out.

You have been breed to be stupid, or rather that is what they will try to make you. If you can't question the world for yourself, and they define the world for you, their truths will always be your realities.

You were meant to be proud. Take pride in the performance you are about to give. You have been cast as the perfect definition of masculinity. Mess up and there is a line of boys being prepped to take your place.

You are supposed to be rough and tough. You are going to be told to be the main provider. Keep your nose to the grindstone and your eyes on the prize, that way you will never see the bodies crumbling next to you, dying from the same disease of complacency you will one day suffer from. If you are lucky, they will train you on how to use your rough and tough personalities to entertain them, because that is all they will ever think you are capable of being. Entertainment.

You have been breed to be mindless, because they fear your mind is limitless. They fear you will dream in colors you can only see. They fear that you know you are powerful beyond belief. That you won't be controllable, manipulable, impulsive, masculine, because masculinity comes in one flavor and that flavor is tasteless. So baby boy, I dare you to be different. They will praise you for your success, but you will always fail alone. But even a shooting star can make someone's wishes come true, so pray on yourself and watch your blessings come through. So dream a dream for yourself, baby boy, never let others dream for you. Dream a dream for yourself, baby boy, and let your dreams come true.

Dreamer

Tell me a story

of the dreams you used to dream

before people started to deem

deem your dreams extreme

for dreams are for children

not adults who seem

seem to not want to grow up

or grow old,

because of the propaganda that streams

from screen to screen

infecting the mainstream

showing the newest way to let your dreams die.

Those who dream

are told they will never be redeemed

for their hours of supreme devotion,

because if life was a play

failure would be the overarching theme

for those who dream

because dreamers

hide behind their childlike fantasies

masking their low-self-esteem

which is an elaborate scheme

but naïve nonetheless.

See, I have a dream

to let my creativity burst at the seams

and flow peacefully like a stream

into every fire hot poem I write

so I can watch the steam rise from the paper

and listen to the screams of people

who seem to be afraid of the fire my dreams might bring.

This is not to boast

or shine a golden beam of glory on myself,

but to scream to the dreamers

to dream, my friends, dream.

So to the dreamers who want to dream

but are afraid to be seen

pursuing their passions, love and soul

dare to be supreme

to be looked at as extreme

because unless you dare to scream

the world may lose the next big thing

that will split the cookie cutter molds

at their seams

allowing for your story

of the dreams you once dreamed

to finally be deemed

deemed beautiful.

Foil

Right in front of left.
Straight line.
One, two, three
One, two, three…
The rigidness in my steps
Contradicts the swaying of my heart.
I charge.

Plunge forward.
My hands shake against the cold metal,
I have been signed up to fight a battle,
but I am fighting in a war that will never end.
Two steps back.
Three steps back.
One step forward,
and thrust.
We dance.
Our movements in sync.
You are the reflection I've longed to see when I look in the mirror.
The swooshing of the air
is the backdrop music for our pounding hearts.

I must learn to love you—
One…
In order to defeat you—
Two…
In order to win—
Three!

Right in front of left

One, two, three
One, two, three
One, two, three
I plunge,
but will I win.

Love Lost

It sits there mocking me
reminding me that it won't quit,
that it won't be broken.
It beats.
Boom

As if it hasn't been scratched.
As if I hadn't tried to silence it,
ignore it…
as if I hadn't wished it would stop…
stop loving.
It beats.
Boom, boom

It laughs at my tears.
It smiles at my pain,
for I am its shield
and it uses me
in hopes of love to gain.
It beats.
Boom, boom, boom

I've tried to drown you in my tears,
but I am your puppet
as you pull on the strings of my soul…
Left arm.
Right arm.
Smile. Dream.
I wish you would just drop me,
But you still beat.

Boom, boom, boom, boom

Pleading,
wishing
hoping
for an end,
but you won't stop.
Can't stop.
You say we can't stop,
and I trust you…
Boom, boom, boom, boom
So I let you beat.

The death of the mask

I am the smile
That is you lie
That hides your tears
When you cry

I am the reflection
You've always wanted to see
For when they see you
They see the lie that is me

I am the mask
They've learned to love
That hides your scars
Like dark clouds above

I am the only one
To have ever seen your face
Though many have tried
Soon all quit the race

You dare not say
What you see
Or how you feel
So you pretend to be me

I am the cave
You call home
Dark and empty I'll always be
Forever I fear you'll aimlessly roam

I am the mask
That prays everyday
That I will break
Causing your insecurities to go away

I am the mask
That no longer wants to lie
I rather the world see your beauty
Even if I must die

Embrace who you are
And the world will see
The person I wish
I could be

They will laugh and tease
may even call you names
but they are the ones
who will always remain the same
lonely and bitter
insecure and weak
constantly pointing their fingers
with no one to blame
but don't be ashamed
for you are beautiful to me
and one day someone will come along and see
why I was willing to die
to let your heart be free.

                      I was the smile
                      That used to lie
                      That hid your tears

when you would cry

I was the reflection
You've always wanted to see
Hoping when they saw you
They would see the lie that was me

I was the mask
They've used to love
That hid your scars
Like dark clouds above

But now I am a memory
Of who you used to be
For without me
You are now truly free

This poem is dedicated to Paul Laurence Dunbar and his poem "we wear the mask". It was time for my mask to come off.

Warrior Nation

We are the warrior nation
A young and new generation
And yet the world knows how we wish to be defined

Education is our birthright
And together we form a tight,
Tight-knit family ready to defend
Until the very end, our birthright.

When we enter we commit,
Commit to do our best
Until we can't do no more
That's when we depend on our brothers
To carry us through the door.

As brothers we unite,
We stick together though sometimes we fight
But we commit ourselves to one another
And stand up for what is right

The life we live is not easy
For we are trying to break the mold
To find the courage to be bold
And find the paths of joy and success

Sometimes we may lose a brother
A warrior from birth, a soldier like no other
But forever and ever he shall be
a warrior, and we shall uphold his legacy

When we enter we commit,
We commit to our family
Our community
To ourselves

We are the warrior nation
A young and new generation
Defining ourselves

~In memory of Emmanuel Sloan, a Boys' Latin warrior

The seed

It's not the dream that defines man,

its man that defines the dream.

So be brave, dear lover

to chase the wind,

spread your arms wide,

dream and pretend

like you did back then.

Touch me and I will shiver.

Name me and I will never go.

Ignore me and I will wait, I shall never die.

Be brave, dear lover

and accept failure as your friend,

for once you learn to love your enemies

that's truly when your heart will mend.

So let the hands of your ticking clock freeze.

Let down your hair, dear lover

and plant thy roots like a tree,

knowing that even the mightiest of trees

start off as seeds.

Unnamed

How do I say goodbye,

when I just learned how to say hello.

I took your hand,

I called you friend,

but my heart called you more.

To know you,

to learn about your world

was all I ever wanted,

but my heart needed more.

I am just a copy,

a shell of who I hope to be,

never wished to be your ruby,

the perfect fusion to become we,

but my heart wished for more.

Adorable and shy

is what my heart said to me,

but I knew we could never be,

so I ignored it,

so my heart yelled more.

If I could

I would.

My heart is telling me I should,

but would it,

could it…

I cant take the risk

though my heart says risk more.

And now I sit,

shifting my head to look at every shadow that passes me by,

hoping to see you again,

wishing I had wanted more.

A prayer for the weary

I walk on this earth

With that pure mustard see faith

I shall never quit

Thoughts

If I knew what I wanted

would it fill my heart with glee,

would my spirit finally be happy,

or am I to be forever empty?

If I knew who you were

would I have the courage to say hello,

would I just flash you a smile,

or sit silently and watch you go?

If I could peer into your heart

would I see that you love me,

or would my heart once again

be my own worse enemy?

If I knew what I wanted

I would have nothing to dream about,

and where is the fun in that?

Imagine

Imagine that the world is her playground

And oh, how I wish I could play

Fighting off vampire pirates

To keep them away

From the tea set

Set for three

A pig

A robot

And me

Until we have to flee

From Mr. Chomp Chomp Chomper

And his gang of hungry hand bandits

Who chase us around the house

I mean world

Trying to tickle our stomachs

Until she becomes a mouse

And I a dragon

Flying through the air

With absolutely no care

Until I am caught by the bad guy

That's when I wait

And wait

For my hero to arrive and set me free

And she does

Except for when she is late

For she had to stop for candy

Or a drink

From the happy giants sink

That drips

Onto the floor

Flooding the land

But good thing were mermaids

Swimming until we find sand

To transform into lions

Clawing at each other

Until I bite down

And pick her up by her shirt

I mean fur

And carry her to the blanket of destiny

And we fly

Over land

And float on the sea

Yelling

Wheeeeeeeee

Until we lose our voices

 And become mimes

Which never happens because she hates silence

So we SCREAMMMMM

And blow hot steam

When I'm her train

Bumping down the track

Going to get her a snack

Of grapes and oranges….

Oranges and grapes

For we are superheroes with long capes

Soaring high

Looking down over her playground

And oh, how I do wish I could play.

~Dedicated to Cianni, the world is yours for the taking.

Curse me

Curse me,
and let me be all you want me to be.
Wrap me around your finger
and whisper to me your lies.
I will treat these scars like artwork
if you will be my painter,
run my finger along each of your creations
and name them after my insecurities.
I will not run or try and hide,
just lay me down by the river
and let my dreams drift away.
Just lay me down by the river
and I will sink to the bottom and stay.
I will kiss your poisoned lips
and with my last breath
say I love you,
if this is truly love.

I am the poem

They ask why my poetry is dark,

why there are tear stains

where words once were,

and yet somehow they understand

that my paper is my armor,

my words my sword,

and I,

the fragile emotional being

dwelling within them.

My words carry the burdens

I could not bare

for they have seen where,

where I am going

and they hope I get there,

so they accept my burdens

so that I can smile.

My words know that without them

I would be engulfed by my raging emotions

clawing to be set free,

so my words, they protect me,

protect me from vanity,

insanity,

anger and rage,

so I willingly exist hostage

inside this cage

of poems.

There are times when I can't find the words to say,

so I say nothing,

that is when you should be afraid

for there must be a tear in this paper thin armor

and my emotions are ready to pillage and raid

all those who have taken them for granted,

and so I write,

taming my emotions

with every stroke of my pen

until they are nestled safely

within the confines of a poem.

A poem I wear as armor

to remind myself of why I love,

why I pray,

and cry,

and fight every day,

so go ahead and ask the question

of why my poetry is so sad,

and I will simply smile

and be glad,

glad to tell you about the poem,

the poem that is me.

The Genie's lamp

I am the saddest story ever told,
the one nobody knows about,
and yet always hear.
I'm like trying to count every rain drop
while a storm rages on,
I'm impossible.
I am the needle in the haystack,
overused and misunderstood.
You will never find me.
Call me like a genie,
rub me tenderly,
caress the misfortuned shape of my insecurities
and whisper your wish in my ear.
One, I wish to be loved.
Two, I wish to find love.
Three, I wish to know love,
and then I disappear
back into myself,
pitying those who find me
for they will only find contentment
on their journey to find themselves.
I'm the one with all the answers,
but I'm never asked the right questions,
so I give
and give
and love
and give,
never to know
what it truly means to be remembered,

to be loved,
until I have been used,
abused,
forgotten,
for I am the one who is desired,
but no one ever wants me.
So touch me and set me free
and watch me serve you,
anticipating your affection,
dreaming of my freedom,
wondering when will it be my turn
to see my dreams come true,
my turn for a happy ending,
a happy ending
for the saddest story ever told.

~In memory of Robin Williams

Butterfly

If I had never learned to fly

I wonder if I would still be called beautiful.

I would sit there

starring at you staring at me,

separated only by air,

and yet I could never reach you.

I named you beautiful

and oh, were you so beautiful,

but your beauty

was becoming a fleeting memory

with the touch of his hands.

You love him,

his beauty.

I can see it in your eyes,

for he is your future

hiding deep within your past.

I cried,

consuming my guilt,

as if I could find happiness

in the destruction of everything I once loved,

in destroying myself.
I never noticed that I was lost,
trapped between the world and myself,
two forces slowly closing in on me
hoping to see me break,
and so I tried,
tried to find the flaws I wish existed
to explain why I had missed,
missed your love.
I emerged,
never realizing I had been submerged
under the ever rising tides of my fears.
I emerge,
staring at you staring at me,
and yet he was still in your eyes,
so I jumped,
nothing between us but air
and I no longer cared
about the outcome,
until my wings began to flap.
My wings began to flap…
when did I get wings?

You stared,

not knowing what to do,

for now I could simply fly to you,

but,

but I couldn't,

so I flew right by you

stealing one final glance

at the one I once knew,

the one I wanted to love,

the one staring at me,

wondering

if I should have landed.

The Fallen Star

As you wrap yourself

snuggly in the comfort of your sheets

I come to life,

starring through curious eyes

as you slowly drift

further and further away

into a reality only you can call home,

and I wonder

as my light softly caresses your face

if you ever dream of me.

Be my siren!

Sing the songs of my destruction,

and let them be the melodies to nourish my soul,

as I lean over the edge, looking into the crystal clear water,

hoping to find myself hidden behind my reflection.

I stand on the bones of my ancestors,

eager to hear your songs,

but too naive to hear what you are saying.

You whisper my name softly,

inviting me to my death, and I walk.

One foot in front of the other,

listening to the bones shatter under my feet,

as if with each crack

that echoes across this deep blue abyss,

it's someone warning me of what's to come.

Begging me to not let go.

But I welcome you with open arms,

wanting your songs to draw me closer,

until it's too late to realize I have drowned.

So sing, sweet siren,

until the deed is done,

until I have felt the kiss of deaths icy lips.

The kiss from you.

And maybe then I will be free.

But you have stopped singing,

and yet your song rings in my ears.

Making me wish I have met you.

Embraced you.

Loved you.

Instead, I've let you go.

Angel at midnight

They say it was ironic

that I meet an angel during the witching hour.

You did not float in on soaring wings,

no trumpets to mark your arrival.

You stumbled through the halls,

your halo hidden from all,

then you fell.

Smiling,

sending uncertainty through my spine,

clouding my mind

like a thick fog of adrenaline.

I smiled back,

though my body wanted to run.

You spoke,

slurring your words as if my

ears could only hear

superficial sentences about my mundane existence.

I nodded,

for your words had more meaning then I was ready to comprehend.

Hello, was all you said,

yet, I knew your greeting meant more.

Hello, was all you said,

until you found the core of my existence,

kicking down the door

to my heart,

smiling a wickedly menacing grin,

upturning the corners of your lips

to accentuate your beautiful barren eyes.

Hello, I found you

you whispered

and I knew I was trapped

for you had found me.

Not the person I was pretending to be,

but the one you knew was

fighting to be free,

the one I wanted to let die

with no concrete reasons why

other then fear.

You smiled,

placing your icy smooth hands on my arm.

Hello, I found you and now you are free.

I nodded,

not understanding the formation of your words

as they fell to the floor,

like concrete flowers,

hoping I would still see their beauty

and take a moment to smell them.

You turned,

stumbling away,

your wings dragging behind you,

leaving me alone

with nothing

but this poem.

The ugly duckling

Quack little duck quack

And tell me who you want to be…

One day I might be beautiful,

and oh, I imagine what I would see

when I finally look in the river

and see what I've longed to be.

Some things are hard to write about,

too abstract for the pen to comprehend,

but let this be my first attempt

at telling my story.

They act like this is what I wanted,

to be an anomaly,

outcasted from society,

all beast

only to imagine what is beauty.

Quack little duck quack

And tell me who you want to be…

I will never be

what you want me to be

and that is my reality.

One day I am told I'll be a swan,

beautiful,

marveled at,

not because of my aesthetic qualities,

but because I am me.

One day I might be beautiful,

and oh, I imagine what you will see

when you finally open your eyes

and see I was always beautiful as me.

Quack little duck quack

And tell me who you want to be…

I want to be no one else

then little ole me.

The caged bird

I wonder if she ever wishes to be free…

locked away,

forced to be a prisoner,

turning

and spinning

and chirping

and singing

to the rhythm of the beating sun,

but at night

free to dream

and sing.

I wonder how long it took her

to learn how to pretend,

to pretend to love her cage

hopping along her perch singing

as if she is happy

as if she is free,

but I hear the pain in her voice

when she sings alone

starring through the bars

out into the world.

I wonder if she ever cries,

collecting her tears

and hanging them from the roof of her cage

watching them dangle,

wishing upon them,

pretending they were stars.

I wonder if she was ever free

soaring above the tree tops,

dancing a duet with the wind,

singing until her voice falters

and she sings silently with glee.

Sometimes I cry for her

wondering how sad it must be

living your life for other people,

never being free,

then I smile,

wondering what she would think of me.

Maybe one day we will meet,

and I wonder the stories she might tell ,

the things she might say.

I wouldn't speak,

afraid she might think my words a trick,

thinking I am mocking her,

so I'd just stare

and imagines the things we could talk about.

Sometimes I just sit,

close my eyes

and listen to her sing,

as I call back to her

sing my caged bird,

sing,

I am pretty

Oh, I am perfect

I am pretty

I am free—

~In memory of Harper Lee.~

The mocking bird

I wonder if she ever wishes to be free…

forced to be a shadow of someone else's words.

I wonder if she ever tries to stop speaking,

constricting her throat,

trying to trap someone else's voice inside her,

until her body collapses

and her words are

reshaped into something,

something more beautiful.

Isn't she a pretty bird,

pretty bird.

Listen to her sing,

sing.

She will always be perfect,

perfect.

She will never leave,

she wants to leave.

I wonder if she ever cries,

singing out to God

asking why was she made this way.

Who would want to live

under the presence

of someone else's control.

Who wouldn't want to be free…

Sometimes I cry for her,

and even still,

sometimes I laugh

wondering what she would think of me.

Perhaps one day I will meet her.

She'll fly in through the window,

resting gently on the window seal

and I'd just stare,

unaware of the right words to say

for anything she'll say

would be an embodiment

of my own perceptions about her existence.

So I'd just stare

and imagine what she would say

if she could speak.

I wonder if she knows she is voiceless,

If she ever tries to find herself

in the words of other people.

I wonder if she even cares.

Sometimes I just sit,

close my eyes

and listen to her sing,

as I call back to her

sing my mocking bird,

sing,

I am pretty

Oh, I am perfect

I am pretty

I am free—

~In memory of Maya Angelou.~

The girl no one knows

She glares

twirling the cigarette between her fingers.

The smoke,

tumbling across her body,

crashing against her form

like a wave,

slowly rising,

cuffing her face,

rolling off of her cheeks,

as it rises into the air

only to disappear

from her existence.

Outrunning time

Her hands

crept slowly forward,

mechanically,

Inching closer and closer,

hoping to finally feel my embrace,

or perhaps

she just wanted to mock our existence,

as if with every wave of her hand

she was recounting the story of our friendship.

One,

Our beginning

the day our friendship

showed a shadow of its existence,

whispering that our road would be long

so keep strong.

Two,

The encounter,

the fierceness of your lips,

the aggression hiding,

nestled soundly under your tongue.

I saw the kindness in your hands,

the compassion in your movements,

the truth behind your fairytale,

and I wanted to be there.

Three,

The call,

the ringing of my phone

telling me that our dance has begun

with midnight calls,

laughs,

tears,

hearing in your voice

that our stars were born

to dance together in the night,

as the moon

softly sung our song.

Four,

The fall from grace,

our resignation from running life's race,

our first punches thrown,

and as the day turned night

we thought we would never see the sun again.

Five,

And this hurts,

this decent from our pedestals

to the floor,

Jack and Jill,

wandering around together,

starring up at her moving hands,

praying our time will never run out.

Six,

Half way through

though I hope,

pray,

time will never be through with us,

with you.

Seven

Eight

Nine

all lost to her hands

to her smile

her embrace

and how I wish she could lose her wings

and forget how to fly

Ten,

And he was gone

hidden somewhere

in the metallic softness of her face

engulfed by the very thing

we thought we'd never run out of

Eleven,

I can hear

the echoes of your voice

with every second that trickles by.

Twelve,

and I stare up at the clock,

wondering if you will ever come back,

or if time

has finally caught up to us.

Perception

Through my camera

the world is beautiful

for my camera finds the beauty,

and I

simply click.

        He doubts that I—

        his eye

        is capable of seeing beauty

        through life's blurry gaze,

        and so

        he places barriers around me

        in hopes I can see

        the world as he dreams it to be.

Click.

He looks through me,

hoping to find the beauty in his life.

They say a picture

is worth a thousand words,

and through his eyes,

there's always a story to be told

if only they are willing to listen

to the stories he has to tell.

Lullaby

They say

if you love something

let it go,

and if it returns

its yours forever.

But as I watch you fly away,

flapping your newly earned wings,

not knowing if

they will support the weight of your existence,

not knowing where you are going.

I wonder if you should ever come back,

and so I bow my head and say goodbye

and sing this lullaby

to you,

knowing you'll never hear it.

Punch like a man

His voice deepened

telling her to tighten her fist

and punch like a man,

as if echoes of his patriarchal upbringing

crept out of his mouth,

and slowly crawled it's way into her existence.

She smiles,

his words a jumbled melody,

lost to the sweetest sounds of her innocence,

as if she could change her gender

with each strike she landed

against his aged, worn down feeble barriers.

As if she would be anything

but herself.

She punched,

her small hands

engulfed in the shadow

of where his hands once were,

and smiled

as she watched his walls fall down.

Colored free

I wonder,

if they knew the color of my soul

would they accept me,

or reject me,

as if that knowledge

would change my existence,

for I am

a young man

who has been

colored, free.

The tears that nurture

There was a time

I would have wasted my tears

as if you deserved them,

but now,

I covet them as if

they are jewels

reminding me of just

how special I am,

my worth.

I let them fall,

watering the ground

beneath my feet,

the same ground you spit at,

while I listen

to you laugh

expecting me to quit,

but with every tear

that falls

I grow

stronger,

bigger,

my roots deeper,

better,

and you will wonder

what my secret is,

and I will just stand tall

knowing there was a time

that I would have wasted my tears on you

as if you deserved them,

but not anymore.

Formless

When I look in the mirror

I am never the person

other people see.

They say I should get in shape

as if the circle is not a shape

pivotal to our existence.

I would love to sit back,

smiling,

 as they try and

drive their cars with triangular wheels,

for they don't see

that beauty is subjective,

and yet it's their objective to try

and pollute my subconscious

with their vision

of my image

seen through their blurry and disfigured eyes,

hoping that one day

I'll rise

to their expectations of a superficial figure

that has been pieced together

with their favorite physical attributes,

as if my perfect mosaic form

would compensate for

their negligence

in leaving me empty.

At least I'd be beautiful.

My Secret

I wonder if you

can see through my smile,

these laughs,

and question

the sparkle in my eye

every time I try and lie,

to side step my feelings,

as if I was crisscrossing

through this maze of emotions

chalked onto the street before us

like I'm hop-scotching my way

one step closer out of your life

…..

or into it.

I tried

entering into another's dreams,

hoping we could be

the beautiful reflections of our past,

struck frozen

on the surface of these black mirrors

we cant seem to let go of,

and it was beautiful,

magical,

simply a distorted image

that I would have claimed to be real,

until I found your smile

outlining the letters of their name,

and I knew

I wasn't over you,

and so I push

and push

you further away

like the rising tide,

hoping that one day

it too can walk upon the land

and see where the green grass grows,

but knows it never can,

and so it thrashes and pushes

and clashes

against the sand,

hoping that through the pain

someone can see its sorrow,

it's longing,

my lon—

but I won't say it

not even a whisper in the wind

for you

my friend

are more valuable

then

taking the risk—

and so I sit and smile,

laugh and giggle for a good while

knowing the comfort of having you as a friend

is better than losing you

and this being

our end.

A Prayer for the Phoenix

My magic

does not resonate with my pure being,

but with the tragedy of my death

and the prayers for my redemption,

my resurrection.

They rather watch my ascent

from the ashes

of my failures,

rather then watch me soar and succeed.

I spread my red wings,

the depths of my fire

captivates those who know me

and scares those who don't.

Some call me the exception,

but I know I am the rule,

so watch as I burn through the sky

and make a wish,

whisper a prayer,

knowing my death is not in vain

for my spirit will always reappear

and I too,

shall rise!

~In memory of Jevon O'Neal

www.ingramcontent.com/pod-product-compliance
Lightning Source LLC
Chambersburg PA
CBHW060814050426
42449CB00008B/1659